I ♥♥ Jesus

Faith Hope Love

"Blessed are those who hunger and thirst for righteousness, for they will be filled."
Matthew 5:6

Dont forget to tear your bleed sheet!
Head to the back of this book to find.

My friends ♥ Jesus

This awesome book belongs to:

_____

Are you ready to have some fun?
Get your crayons and let's go!

we ♡ our friends !

Let's name some friends

....
....
....
....

do you know this song?
let's sing!

Jesus loves the little children,
all the children of the world.
Red, and yellow, black, and white,
they are precious in His sight.
Jesus loves the little children of the world

We say grace to Him, because we are thankful.
Let's pray!
'God is great, God is good,
Let us thank Him for our food.
By His hands we are fed.
Thank you Lord for our daily bread.'

Can you find these words?

Jesus loves me

S	L	H	R	M	P	O	P	L	H	S	L	S	L
H	U	H	U	E	O	S	H	A	S	U	B	B	S
E	T	F	O	I	H	T	M	H	I	S	E	M	H
P	A	S	I	L	I	H	H	I	N	E	R	A	C
H	D	R	A	M	Y	H	B	E	G	J	O	L	R
E	L	O	E	H	E	L	H	B	R	C	H	D	U
R	I	R	H	E	E	L	F	F	O	R	H	E	H
D	H	B	R	R	L	E	P	E	I	E	O	A	C
J	C	M	S	L	B	O	R	H	Y	C	P	S	E
I	O	C	S	G	I	L	F	A	T	H	E	R	D
I	B	Y	O	L	B	S	T	T	S	I	R	H	C
H	J	E	R	O	P	E	A	C	E	B	O	E	C
M	E	L	C	V	V	H	F	A	I	T	H	O	R
H	S	I	M	E	E	P	P	O	I	D	O	G	C

HOLY
CROSS
HOPE
BIBLE
SING
PEACE
JOY
FAITH
CHILD
FATHER
CHURCH
JESUS
SHEPHERD
MOTHER
LAMB
LOVE
GOD
CHRIST

YOU GO GiRL!

WOW!

U got this!!

We love Sunday school. We sing songs and learn about Jesus.

What is your favorite part of Sunday School?

fun fact:
    did you know that doodling can
        promote relaxation?
        do some doodles!

What is your favorite thing to do with your Dad, Grandpa, or Uncle??

YOU
GO
GIRL

Let's doodle today!

My brother, sister and I enjoy walking to Church.

doodles and songs!

Jesus loves me this I know,
for the Bible tells me so. Little ones to Him
belong, they are weak but He is strong.
Yes, Jesus loves me, Yes Jesus loves me,
Yes Jesus loves me, the Bible tells me so.

all my friends sing...!

This lil' light of mine, I'm gonna let it shine.

This lil' light of mine, I'm gonna let it shine

This lil' light of mine, I'm gonna let it shine

Let it shine, let it shine, let it shine!

let's color our doodle!

Jesus

Do you know John 3:16 ?

friends are awesome!
What fun things do you do with friends?

"Jesus said, 'Let the little children come to me, and do not hinder them, for the kingdom of heaven belongs to such as these."
Matthew 19:14 (NIV)

"The Lord is good to all; He has compassion on all He has made." – Psalm 145:9 (NIV)

Do you have a pet? What is their name?

︵︵︵︵︵︵︵︵︵︵︵︵︵︵︵︵︵︵︵

Do you know who died on the cross for our sins?

Hint: He was God's only son

If you're happy and you know it clap your hands
(repeat)

If you're happy & you know it, then your face will surely show it. If you're happy and you know it clap your hands!

Awesome!

My
bestie

Ready for camp? Are your friends going?

Let;s have fun and color!
Wanna memorize a Bible verse!
"We love because He first loved us."
1 John 4:19 (NIV)

Let us sing so Heaven can hear us!

The B-I-B-L-E, Yes, that's the book for me. I stand alone on the Word of God, The B-I-B-L-E.

You have a beautiful Heart filled with joy for Jesus!

Spell DoG backward...what is the word?

"Don't let anyone look down on you because you are young, but set an example for the believers in speech, in conduct, in love, in faith and in purity"

1 Timothy 4:12

STORY OF MY LIFE

During summer break, do you like to ride bikes with your friends?

_____

_____

_____

"Peace I leave with you; my peace I give you. I do not give to you as the world gives. Do not let your hearts be troubled and do not be afraid." - John 14:27

My friends love wearing cute dresses to
Church! Lets color these cute outfits!

What is your favorite song to sing at Church?

Everyday you are loved by your family and by God!

"Rejoice always, pray continually, give thanks in all circumstances; for this is God's will for you in Christ Jesus."
1 Thessalonians 5:16-18

"But Jesus said 'Let the little children come to me and do not hinder them, for to such belongs the kingdom of heaven." Matthew 19:14

He is risen

Can you count how many hearts are in this doodle?
Trick: color the hearts..it's easier to count!

Do you have a favorite flavor of ice cream?

What do you love most about your Mom?
Her kisses? Her Hugs? Her cookies?

_____○
_____○
_____○
_____○

YaY! Do you laugh with your friends?

So Good

Let's draw some hearts!

Kittens are so playful, so soft & fluffy. Did you know that cats purr because they are happy? Can you purr like a kitten? puuurrrrr!

Swinging is so fun! Could you swing all day?

Let's memorize another Bible verse!

"Happy are the people whose God is the LORD!"
Psalm 144:15

GIRL squad

Sister squad

Ready for a joke?

Why did the bicycle fall over?
answer:
Because it was two-tired!

Ha Ha Ha Ha Ha Ha

Word search!

Q	K	C	T	P	U	C	O	O	L	P	W	K	D
C	W	H	D	G	H	V	A	Z	B	R	V	Q	O
R	H	P	S	R	S	L	S	W	E	E	T	E	O
F	J	O	Q	L	E	Y	S	J	S	T	H	C	D
U	L	X	U	A	C	S	M	K	T	E	O	E	L
Y	S	U	A	U	R	O	S	S	F	N	M	C	E
W	P	I	D	G	E	X	Q	U	R	D	E	G	S
S	P	R	N	H	T	K	W	P	I	A	W	G	W
C	W	U	A	G	S	D	W	P	E	N	O	I	C
H	Z	S	S	Y	N	S	Y	O	N	C	R	R	P
U	D	L	T	I	E	D	B	R	D	E	K	L	T
R	S	O	X	U	D	R	D	T	T	T	L	Y	V
C	O	V	H	K	D	J	O	K	E	S	K	U	A
H	K	E	K	B	C	Y	U	X	H	E	A	R	T

BESTFRIEND
HEART
CHURCH
SWEET
GIRLY
SQUAD
PRAYER
COOL
SUPPORT
STUDY
DRESS
LAUGH
HOMEWORK
PRETEND
LOVE

fun & games

My big sister went on a mission trip to Mexico too
with friends from Church. COOL

"Trust in the Lord with all your heart and lean not on your own understanding; in all your ways submit to Him, and He will make your paths straight."
Proverbs 3:5-6

Made in the USA
Las Vegas, NV
22 October 2024

10136348R00059